THE
Lincoln
Memorial

Published by The Child's World®
1980 Lookout Drive • Mankato, MN 56003-1705
800-599-READ • www.childsworld.com

Acknowledgments
The Child's World®: Mary Berendes, Publishing Director
The Design Lab: Design
Jody Jensen Shaffer: Editing
Red Line Editorial: Photo Research

Photo credits
Wendy Kaveney Photography/Shutterstock Images, cover;
Currier & Ives/Library of Congress, 5; Library of Congress, 6;
Harris & Ewing/Library of Congress, 9, 10; Brand X Pictures,
13; Carol M. Highsmith/Library of Congress, 14; PhotoDisc_
USLndmks, 17; Shutterstock Images, 18; Popperfoto/Getty
Images, 21

ISBN 9781623239572
LCCN 2013947399

Printed in the United States of America
Mankato, MN
November, 2013
PA02189

ABOUT THE AUTHOR

Frederic Gilmore enjoys traveling, reading, playing games with his wife, and wrestling with his five children. He and his family live in Eagan, Minnesota.

TABLE OF CONTENTS

A Fallen President

On April 14, 1865, the President of the United States, Abraham Lincoln, went to a play at Ford's Theater in Washington, DC. While President Lincoln and his wife watched the play, a man named John Wilkes Booth approached Lincoln from behind. Booth pointed a gun at President Lincoln and shot him in the back of the head. Booth then ran from the theater. While Booth made his escape, President Lincoln lay dying. He died the next day.

John Wilkes Booth killed the 16th President of the United States. He killed the man who had freed the slaves. He killed the man who had gone to war to save the Union we call the United States. People around the world were shocked. The people of the United States were in **mourning**. The leader of the United States was dead.

This drawing shows John Wilkes Booth firing the shot that killed President Lincoln.

Thousands of people lined the streets of Washington, DC to watch Lincoln's funeral procession.

A President to Be Remembered

After Abraham Lincoln's death, many people thought it was important to remember him. They wanted to remember Lincoln's actions as well as the **virtues** that he believed were important. Different people had different ideas about how best to remember and show respect for Lincoln's achievements.

On February 19, 1911, the United States Congress created the Lincoln Memorial Commission. This group of people chose a location in Washington DC, called Potomac Park, for the memorial. This site had a good view of the White House, the Washington Monument, and the Capitol building. The commission asked architects to draw ideas for the memorial. Henry Bacon was an architect in New York. His idea was presented to Congress and approved.

Building the Memorial

Workers began preparing the site for the memorial on February 12, 1914. The date was important because it was the 105th anniversary of Abraham Lincoln's birth.

The location chosen for the new memorial was swampy and wet. The workers had to build a platform strong enough to support the weight of the building. The platform was 14 feet (4 meters) high, 257 feet (78 meters) long, and 187 feet (57 meters) wide—almost as big as a football field. Dirt was put around the platform to form a mound. After a year of work on the platform base, the first stone of the memorial building was set in place on February 12, 1915.

This photo shows the Lincoln Memorial early on during its construction.

Here you can see the memorial before it had a roof built.

Henry Bacon's plans for the memorial building were modeled after very old Greek architecture. **Marble** was used to build most of the memorial. The memorial building has a huge marble roof supported by large marble columns. The columns are 44 feet (13 meters) high and more than 7 feet (2 meters) across. Thirty-six columns support the roof. That was the number of states in the Union when Lincoln was president. Lincoln fought the Civil War to keep the 36 states united as one country.

Different kinds of marble as well as other hard stones were used to construct the memorial. These stones were brought from many different states. The floor of the memorial is made of Tennessee Pink marble. The columns and the outside of the building are Colorado Yule marble. The walls inside the memorial are Indiana limestone. The ceiling is made from **translucent** Alabama marble. When the memorial building was completed, it was as tall as a nine-story building.

The Statue of Lincoln

Bacon's plan also called for a statue of Lincoln to be placed in the center of the building near the back. But Bacon was an architect, not an artist.

To build the statue of Lincoln, the Memorial Commission chose Daniel Chester French. French was an American **sculptor** who had studied in Paris, France. He was considered to be the best American sculptor at the time. The Lincoln Memorial Commission asked French to sculpt a statue of Lincoln that would be at least 10 feet (3 meters) tall. Bacon and French decided that a statue of Lincoln sitting down would best represent the difficult times the former president endured.

French made a small model of the statue and showed it to the commission. The members of the commission approved the idea for the statue on February 28, 1916.

French and Bacon chose to have Lincoln seated rather than standing.

IN THIS TEMPLE
AS IN THE HEARTS OF THE PEOPLE
FOR WHOM HE SAVED THE UNION
THE MEMORY OF ABRAHAM LINCOLN
IS ENSHRINED FOREVER

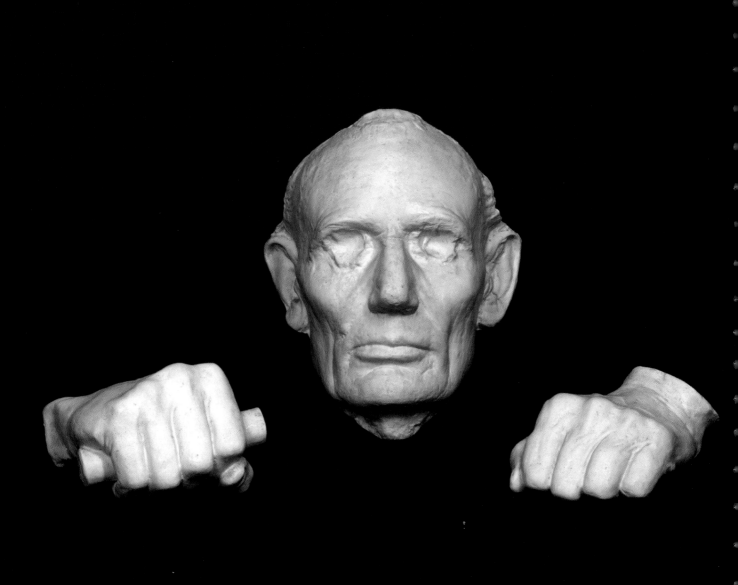

These are the plaster casts that Leonard Volk made.

The Life Mask

To create a realistic and lifelike statue of the president, French used photographs and a "life mask" of Lincoln. The life mask was actually a plaster mold of the president's face that was made back when Lincoln was alive. The mask was created by an artist named Leonard Volk, who met with Lincoln in 1860 when Lincoln was a **candidate** for the presidency. Volk wrote down detailed measurements of Lincoln's upper body. He made plaster molds of Lincoln's hands, too.

French used Volk's measurements of Lincoln, the life mask, and the plaster casts of Lincoln's hands to make his statue as lifelike as possible.

The Work Continues

French made plans to begin the final statue of Lincoln that would be the centerpiece of the memorial. At the same time, work on the memorial building slowed in 1917 because the United States had entered World War I. Bacon saw one of French's models of the statue and began to think it was too small for the large memorial building. After comparing photographs of the building and the model of the statue, Bacon and French decided that the statue would have to be much larger than the 10-foot (3-meter) height they had planned.

Bacon and French asked the Lincoln Memorial Commission for permission to make the statue of Lincoln 19 feet (about 6 meters) tall. The commission approved the request.

The size of the memorial building led to the Lincoln statue being made taller.

ABSORBS THE ... FORTH
...ARMS PRESENTED LITTLE THAT IS ... GREAT
...PENDS IS AS UPON WHICH THE ENERGIES
...S TO MYSELF AND WELL KNOWN ALL ELSE PROGRESS OF NEW
...BLY SATISFACTORY AND IT IS I TRUST TO THE PUBLIC
...L WITH HIGH HOPE FOR THE ENCOURAGING TO
...EDICTION IN REGARD TO IT IS FUTURE NO
...ON THE OCCASION CORRESPONDING VENTURED
...IS FOUR YEARS AGO ALL THOUGHTS WER
...XIOUSLY DIRECTED TO AN IMPENDING
...VIL WAR · ALL DREADED IT ~ ALL SOUGH
...AVERT IT · WHILE THE INAUGURAL A
...SS WAS BEING DELIVERED FROM TH
...CE DEVOTED ALTOGETHER TO SAVIN
...UNION WITHOUT WAR INSURGE
...NTS WERE IN THE CITY SEEKING TO D
...Y IT WITHOUT WAR ~ SEEKING TO
...E THE UNION AND DIVIDE

This carving in the Lincoln Memorial is of Lincoln's Second Inaugural Address.

After getting approval for the larger statue, French made another model. He also decided the statue would be carved out of Georgia White marble. But French could not find a big enough piece of marble without any flaws. French would need to put the statue of Lincoln together from pieces of marble.

With the help of **stonecutters** named the Piccirilli brothers, the huge statue of Lincoln was carved out of 28 pieces of perfect marble. The pieces were then placed together like pieces of a puzzle. In May of 1920, the statue of Lincoln was finished and the memorial building was nearing completion.

Two **murals** were painted on the walls inside the memorial. Two of President Lincoln's famous speeches were carved into the walls. Lights were added to allow people to view the memorial at night. Trees and grass were planted around the memorial, too.

The Memorial Completed

The Lincoln Memorial was dedicated during a ceremony on May 30, 1922. The guest of honor at the ceremony was Robert Todd Lincoln, the only living son of former President Lincoln.

Since 1922, many events have occurred at the Lincoln Memorial. The most famous may have been a speech by Dr. Martin Luther King, Jr., on August 28, 1963. From the steps of the Lincoln Memorial, King gave a speech called "I Have a Dream." More than 200,000 people were at the Lincoln Memorial that day to hear him speak.

Today you can visit the Lincoln Memorial. It is located at the west end of a large reflecting pool. At the other end of the pool is the Washington Monument, and behind that is the Capitol dome.

This picture shows Martin Luther King, Jr.,
delivering his "I Have a Dream" speech.

Glossary

candidate (KAN-did-ayt) A candidate is a person who is running in an election. Abraham Lincoln was a candidate for the presidency in 1860 when his life mask was created.

marble (MARB-ul) Marble is a type of stone that is very hard and good for building. Many different types of marble were used in the Lincoln Memorial.

mourning (MORN-ing) Mourning is showing sadness for a person's death. The American people were in mourning after President Lincoln was killed.

murals (MYUR-ulz) A mural is artwork that is made to be an important part of a wall or ceiling. There are two murals inside the Lincoln Memorial.

sculptor (SKULP-tur) A sculptor is a person who makes artwork out of solid objects. Daniel Chester French was the sculptor who made the statue of President Lincoln.

stonecutters (STONE-cut-terz) Stonecutters are people who are skilled at cutting and carving stone. French hired the Piccirilli brothers as stonecutters for the memorial.

translucent (trans-LOO-sent) An object that you cannot see through—but that some light can still pass through—is called translucent. A translucent type of marble was used in the ceiling of the Lincoln Memorial.

virtues (VIR-chooz) A personal quality or trait that people see as being good is called a virtue. President Lincoln had many virtues.

Find Out More

IN THE LIBRARY

Erin, Audrey. *Visit the Lincoln Memorial.* New York: Gareth Stevens, 2012.

Hankins, Chelsey. *The Lincoln Memorial.* New York: Chelsea Clubhouse, 2010.

Nelson, Kristin L. *The Lincoln Memorial.* Minneapolis, MN: Lerner, 2011.

Ruffin, Frances E. *The Lincoln Memorial.* Milwaukee, WI: Weekly Reader Early Learning Library, 2006.

ON THE WEB

Visit our Web site for lots of links about the Lincoln Memorial:
www.childsworld.com/links

Note to Parents, Teachers, and Librarians: We routinely check our Web links to make sure they're safe, active sites—so encourage your readers to check them out!

Index